LTL

3/04

P9-EEN-087

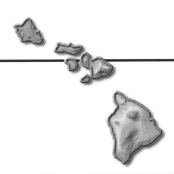

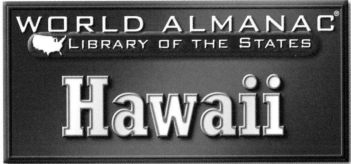

THE ALOHA STATE

by Robin Doak

WORLD ALMANAC® LIBRARY

Please visit our web site at: **www.worldalmanaclibrary.com**
**For a free color catalog describing World Almanac® Library's list of high-quality books
and multimedia programs, call 1-800-848-2928 (USA) or 1-800-387-3178 (Canada).
World Almanac® Library's fax: (414) 332-3567.**

Library of Congress Cataloging-in-Publication Data

Doak, Robin S. (Robin Santos), 1949-
    Hawaii, the Aloha State / by Robin Doak.
        p. cm. — (World Almanac Library of the states)
    Includes bibliographical references and index.
    Summary: Presents the history, geography, people, politics and government,
economy, social life and customs, state events and attractions, and notable
people of Hawaii.
    ISBN 0-8368-5149-8 (lib. bdg.)
    ISBN 0-8368-5320-2 (softcover)
    1. Hawaii—Juvenile literature. [1. Hawaii.] I. Title. II. Series.
DU623.25.D63   2003
996.9—dc21   2002034320

First published in 2003 by
World Almanac® Library
330 West Olive Street, Suite 100
Milwaukee, WI 53212 USA

Copyright © 2003 by World Almanac® Library.

A Creative Media Applications Production
Design: Alan Barnett, Inc.
Copy editor: Laurie Lieb
Fact checker: Joan Vernero
Photo researcher: Linette Mathewson
World Almanac® Library project editor: Tim Paulson
World Almanac® Library editors: Mary Dykstra, Gustav Gedatus, Jacqueline Laks Gorman,
  Lyman Lyons
World Almanac® Library art direction: Tammy Gruenewald
World Almanac® Library graphic designers: Scott M. Krall, Melissa Valuch

Photo credits: pp. 4-5 © David R. Frazier/Danita Delimont, Agent; p. 6 (left) © F. Stuart
Westmoreland/Danita Delimont, Agent; p. 6 (top) © Bruce Coleman; p. 6 (bottom) © ArtToday;
p. 7 (top) © ArtToday; p. 7 (bottom) © Bruce Coleman; p. 9 © North Wind Picture Archives;
p. 10 © North Wind Picture Archives; p. 11 © Photri Inc.; p. 12 © Photri Inc.; p. 13 © North Wind
Picture Archives; p. 14 © Hulton Archive/Getty; p. 15 © AP/Wide World Photos; p. 17 © Jeff
Greenberg/ Danita Delimont, Agent; p. 18 © Walter Bibikow/Danita Delimont, Agent; p. 19
© Walter Bibikow/Danita Delimont, Agent; p. 20 (left to right) © Tim Till, © Bruce Coleman,
© John C. Parker/Positive Images; p. 21 (left to right) © ArtToday, © John C. Parker/Positive
Images, © F. Stuart Westmoreland/Danita Delimont; p. 23 © Bruce Coleman; p. 26 © Bruce
Coleman; p. 27 © ArtToday; p. 29 © Bruce Coleman; p. 30 © Jeff Greenberg; p. 31 (top) © Photri
Inc.; p. 31 (bottom) © AP/Wide World Photos; p. 32 © Bruce Coleman; p. 33 © AP/Wide World
Photos; p. 34 © AP/Wide World Photos; p. 35 © ArtToday; p. 36 © AP/Wide World Photos;
p. 37 (top) © Photri Inc.; p. 37 (bottom) © AP/World Wide Photos; p. 38 © Photri Inc.; p. 39 (all)
© Photri Inc.; p. 40 © Photri Inc.; p. 41 (top) © Photri Inc.; p. 41 (bottom) © AP/Wide World
Photos; pp. 42-43 © North Wind Picture Archives; p. 44 (top) © ArtToday; p. 44 (bottom) © Bruce
Coleman; p. 45 (top) © ArtToday; p. 45 (bottom) © Bruce Coleman

Printed in the United States of America

2 3 4 5 6 7 8 9 07 06 05 04 03

Hawaii

Welcome to Hawaii

Hawaii is unlike any other state in the United States. It is located in the Pacific Ocean about fourteen hundred miles (2,253 kilometers) north of the equator and more than two thousand miles (3,218 km) from California. Hawaii comprises eight main islands and more than 120 islets, reefs, and shoals. The islands, formed millions of years ago by volcanoes, are a tropical paradise, with sandy beaches, lush rain forests, and volcanic peaks.

Hawaii's nickname is the "Aloha State." *Aloha* is a native Hawaiian word that has many meanings. It can mean both "welcome" and "farewell." It can also mean "love to you." For centuries, the hospitable climate and geography of the Hawaiian Islands have welcomed people from around the world.

The first people to settle here were Polynesians who arrived around A.D. 300. The culture developed by these and later Polynesian settlers is still apparent in Hawaii today. Many islanders speak Hawaiian, one of the two official state languages (the other is English). Ancient customs, practices, and foods are still to be found.

As Europeans and Americans arrived in the islands, they began to influence the native culture. The first American settlers were Protestant missionaries who arrived in 1820. They founded churches and schools, but they also banned some native customs. American settlers bought up Hawaiian land and founded sugar and pineapple plantations. They brought thousands of laborers from Asia and other countries to work on the plantations. In 1893, whites in Hawaii overthrew the native government, a monarchy, and declared Hawaii a republic. In 1959, Hawaii became the fiftieth U.S. state.

Today, Hawaii's tropical climate, exotic volcanic landscapes, and unique blend of cultures make it one of the top tourist destinations in the world. Each year, millions of people from the U.S. mainland and around the world come to experience the warmth and magic of the Aloha State.

▶ Map of Hawaii showing the interstate highway system as well as major cities and waterways.

▼ Hawaii is known for its beautiful beaches.

PACIFIC OCEAN

N

Waimea River-
Poomau Stream
KAUAI
Lihue

NIIHAU
Halalii L.
Halulu L.

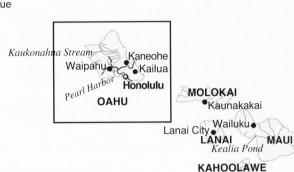

Kaukonahua Stream
Kaneohe
Waipahu
Kailua
Pearl Harbor
Honolulu
OAHU

MOLOKAI
Kaunakakai

Wailuku
Lanai City
LANAI
MAUI
Kealia Pond

KAHOOLAWE

Area of Detail

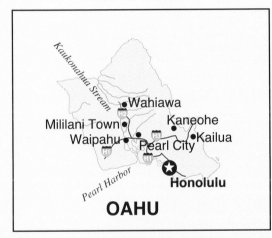

Kaukonahua Stream
Wahiawa
H2
Mililani Town
Kaneohe
Waipahu
H3
Kailua
Pearl City
H1
H1
Honolulu
Pearl Harbor

OAHU

Wailuku R.
Hilo
Kailua-Kona
HAWAII
Captain Cook

SCALE KEY

0   100 Miles

0   100KM

★ Capital

▬ Interstate Highways

Fast Facts

HAWAII (HI), The Aloha State

Entered Union

August 21, 1959 (50th state)

Capital — **Population**

Honolulu 371,657*

*Locations in Hawaii are called "census designated places (CDPs)." Although these areas are not incorporated, they are recognized for census purposes as large urban places. Honolulu CDP has the same boundaries as Honolulu Judicial District within the city and county of Honolulu.

Total Population (2000)

1,211,537 (42nd most populous state)

— *Between 1990 and 2000, the state's population increased 9.3 percent.*

Largest Cities — **Population**

Honolulu 371,657
Hilo 40,759
Kailua 36,513
Kaneohe 34,970
Waipahu 33,108

Land Area

6,423 square miles (16,636 square kilometers) (47th largest state)

State Motto

Ua mau ke ea o ka aina i ka pono — *Hawaiian for* "The life of the land is perpetuated in righteousness."

State Song

"Hawaii Ponoi" ("Hawaii's Own"), *lyrics by King David Kalakaua, music by Henry Berger, adopted in 1967.*

State Bird

Nene, or Hawaiian goose — *The nene, a relative of the Canada goose, is an endangered species.*

State Marine Mammal

Humpback whale — *A large group of humpback whales spend their winters off the coast of Hawaii.*

State Flower

Pua aloalo, or yellow hibiscus

State Tree

Kukui, or candlenut

State Gem

Black coral

State Dance

Hula — *The hula is a sacred dance that was used by early Hawaiians to pass on stories and legends.*

Official Languages

English and Hawaiian

Haleakala National Park, *Maui*
This park includes Haleakala Observatory on Puu Ulaula summit, a satellite-tracking station, and Haleakala Crater, the world's largest inactive volcanic crater.

Hawaii Volcanoes National Park, *Island of Hawaii*
Two active volcanoes in the park, Mauna Loa and Kilauea, continue to erupt. Kilauea, which began erupting again in 1983, is the world's most active volcano. Its lava flows continue to add land to Hawaii.

Pearl Harbor, *Oahu*
Located about 6 miles (9.7 kilometers) west of Honolulu, Pearl Harbor was the site of a Japanese attack on the United States in 1941. The USS *Arizona* Memorial is found here.

For other places and events, see p. 44.

BIGGEST, BEST, AND MOST

- Mount Waialeale, on Kauai, is the wettest spot in the United States. The area receives an annual average rainfall of 460 inches (1,168 centimeters).

- Mauna Kea, on the island of Hawaii, is the tallest mountain in the world when measured from its underwater base to its tip. The inactive volcano measures nearly 33,142 feet (10,102 meters).

- Hilo, on the island of Hawaii, is the southernmost city in the United States.

- The 3,300-foot (1,006-m) sea cliffs of Molokai's north coast are the tallest in the world.

STATE FIRSTS

- **1902** The first Pacific cable linked Hawaii and California.
- **1959** Hawaiian Hiram Fong became the first Asian American in the U.S. Senate.
- **1972** Hawaii became the first state to ratify the Equal Rights Amendment.

Hawaii's Unofficial State Fish

The *humu-humu-nuku-nuku-apua'a* is Hawaii's unofficial state fish. Also known as the Hawaiian triggerfish, this small, colorful fish can be found hiding in the reefs and lagoons off Hawaii's coast. In 1985, the humu-humu-nuku-nuku-apua'a won a statewide contest to be named Hawaii's official state fish. It served a five-year term as state fish, but a new contest has not been held since then.

Eye on the Sky

Mauna Kea, the highest spot in Hawaii, is the perfect place to peek into the clear night sky. As a result, a number of observatories and astronomical research facilities are located on top of the inactive volcano. One facility, the W. M. Keck Observatory, features the two Keck telescopes, the largest optical and infrared telescopes in the world. Each telescope stands eight stories tall and weighs 300 tons (305

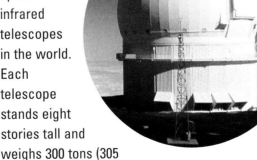

metric tons). Over the years, these big telescopes have photographed comets crashing into Jupiter, mapped faraway galaxies, and recorded other important events in objects in outer space.

A Melting Pot of Cultures

> It is essential that none of the other great powers shall secure these islands. Such a possession would not consist with our safety and with the peace of the world.
>
> — *President Benjamin Harrison,*
> *from a special message to Congress, 1893*

Between A.D. 300 and A.D. 600, people from the Marquesas Islands in the central Pacific Ocean began arriving in Hawaii. These Polynesian people paddled more than two thousand miles northwest in big, double-hulled canoes to get to their new home. Carrying seeds of trees, fruits, and vegetables with them, they planted bananas, breadfruit, coconuts, sugarcane, and sweet potatoes in their new homeland. They also brought pigs, dogs, and poultry to the islands.

Around A.D. 1000, a new group of settlers arrived from Tahiti, another Polynesian island. The Tahitians took control of the Hawaiian Islands, settling in villages along the coastlines. Villagers fished in the oceans and farmed the land, growing crops of taro, a starchy herb. They boiled and mashed taro to make a sticky, paste-like substance called poi.

Soon, each of the main islands had its own rulers. The kings — and queen — who would rule Hawaii for more than eight centuries, until 1893, were descended from the Tahitians. When Europeans first arrived in 1778, there were about 300,000 Hawaiians living on the islands.

European Exploration

In January 1778, Captain James Cook became the first European to reach Hawaii. Cook, an English explorer, landed on the island of Kauai. He was greeted by the native islanders as the god Lono, one of the four major Hawaiian gods. Legends told that the fair-skinned Lono would come to Hawaii on a "floating island." The Hawaiians believed that Cook's big ship, the *Resolution*, was the floating island.

Cook named the islands the Sandwich Islands, after his patron John Montagu, the fourth Earl of Sandwich.

DID YOU KNOW?

Captain James Cook was a famous explorer before he ever laid eyes on the Hawaiian Islands. In 1768, Cook commanded a voyage of discovery that claimed New Zealand and Australia for England. During a three-year trip that began in 1772, Cook became the first explorer to cross the Antarctic Circle. He also discovered a number of previously uncharted Pacific islands. Cook's third and final great voyage brought him to the Hawaiian islands. On this trip, Cook hoped to discover a Northwest Passage across North America that connected the Pacific and Atlantic Oceans. Cook's final voyage, however, ended in failure and death.

The captain spent two weeks in Hawaii, trading iron and trinkets from England for supplies. Then he and his crew headed north to explore the area. When Cook returned to the islands in January 1779, the Hawaiians no longer believed he was Lono. The English captain was killed during a battle between his crew and the Hawaiians.

Cook's expedition opened the door to European exploration and settlement in Hawaii. People from a number of countries in Europe made their home on the island of Oahu, near what is now Honolulu. These new arrivals influenced native Hawaiian customs. They also brought diseases and alcohol. The native population began to decline.

American Settlement

Soon after Cook's death, the great warrior Kamehameha began his quest to unite the Hawaiian Islands. In 1782, Kamehameha seized control of the island of Hawaii from his cousin. Over the next three decades, the great chief gained control of the rest of the main islands. The rule of Kamehameha I, also called Kamehameha the Great, was a time of prosperity for the islands. Kamehameha began the

▼ An illustration depicts the death of Captain James Cook on February 14, 1779. Cook was killed on the island of Hawaii during a skirmish with the natives there.

first of Hawaii's industries, sandalwood trading. Sandalwood was a wood that was highly prized in Asia. American merchants would buy the wood in Hawaii and take it to China to sell.

In 1819, American whaling ships began making regular stops in Hawaii for fresh fruits and other supplies. Sometimes, Hawaiian men were recruited as crew members. Two of the busiest Hawaiian ports were Honolulu on Oahu and Lahaina on Maui. The two towns quickly adapted to serve the whalers' needs. Soon, shops, taverns, and hotels lined the streets.

In 1820, a group of fourteen Protestant missionaries arrived from Boston, Massachusetts. The first Americans to settle in Hawaii, they hoped to convert the Hawaiian natives to Christianity and to "civilize" them. To the missionaries, this meant making the natives more like themselves. Led by the Reverend Hiram Bingham, the missionaries banned alcohol, gambling, the practice of marrying more than one person at a time, and working or horse riding on Sundays. They also banned the hula, a dance that was an important part of native Hawaiian culture. To the Hawaiians, the hula was more than just entertainment. This sacred dance was a means of passing on native stories and legends. The missionaries also created the first written Hawaiian alphabet, based on the way the Hawaiian language sounded. The alphabet contained just twelve letters. One of the first books translated into Hawaiian was the Bible.

▼ During the 1870s, Honolulu was a bustling port town and the capital of the Sandwich Islands.

Americans Take Control

In 1835, William Hooper of Boston leased a 980-acre (397-hectare) plot of land on Kauai from Kamehameha III and began the first permanent sugar plantation in Hawaii. Within thirty years, sugar would completely change Hawaii's economy and its future. By then, large sugar plantations were operating on four of the main islands.

In 1848, Kamehameha III passed the Great *Mahele*, or division. This land division allowed commoners to buy land for the first time. The people who benefited the most from the new law were Americans and Europeans. American missionaries and their sons began buying huge tracts of the best land. By the end of the 1800s, foreigners owned four times as much land as the Hawaiian natives, much of it huge sugar plantations.

On the U.S. mainland, "Sandwich Island sugar" became very popular. During the California Gold Rush (1849–1851), Hawaiian sugar was shipped to San Francisco to sweeten the coffee of miners hoping to strike it rich. The demand for Hawaiian sugar skyrocketed during the Civil War (1861–1865), when the North no longer had access to sugar from the South. Even though Hawaiian planters had to pay expensive duties, or taxes, to ship their goods into U.S. harbors, they still made a good profit. In 1875, Hawaii and the United States signed the Treaty of Reciprocity. This special trade agreement allowed Hawaii to export sugar to the mainland without having to pay duties. In exchange, the United States received long-term rights to Pearl Harbor on Oahu. The trade treaty brought great wealth to the Hawaiian islands, especially to the plantation owners.

Native Hawaiians were the first people to work on the sugar plantations. As the industry grew, plantation owners, who needed more workers, began bringing immigrants from Asia to work for a certain number of years. This arrangement was called contract labor.

Kamehameha I

Kamehameha I, known as Kamehameha the Great, was the first ruler of all the Hawaiian Islands. Born around 1758 on the island of Hawaii, Kamehameha was a nephew of the island's chief. He may have been one of the warriors who watched Captain James Cook arrive in 1778. After the death of his uncle in 1782, the great warrior seized control of Hawaii. By 1810, the rest of the Hawaiian islands had either been conquered or had acceded to his rule. Kamehameha reigned over a united Hawaii, ending regional warfare and creating new laws for all the islands. One of the new laws banned human sacrifice. Kamehameha also encouraged trade with the Europeans and Americans, which made his kingdom rich and prosperous. Kamehameha died on May 8, 1819, and was succeeded by his twenty-two-year-old son, Kamehameha II. The great king's remains were buried in secret, and today Kamehameha's final resting place is still a mystery.

The first group of immigrants to work on the plantations was the Chinese. From 1852 to 1856, thousands of Chinese migrated to Hawaii. Many decided to stay after they had completed their contracts. The largest group of immigrants was the Japanese. Workers began arriving from Japan as early as 1868, but Japanese immigration soared from 1885 to 1900. In just two years, 300,000 Japanese workers arrived in Hawaii. All of these immigrants added new, unique elements to Hawaii's culture. Other immigrant groups that changed the face of Hawaii included Portuguese, Puerto Rican, Korean, and Filipino workers.

The Republic of Hawaii

As sugar became more important to Hawaii's economy, the plantation owners gained more power. Soon, five companies owned all of the plantations throughout the islands. Known as the Big Five, the companies' owners also controlled banking, trade, and local government in most areas of Hawaii. The native monarchy had lost most of its power.

Conflict arose between the Big Five and the Hawaiian monarchy in 1891. That year, Queen Liliuokalani took the

▼ Beginning in 1852, thousands of immigrants came to Hawaii from China. Here, Chinese workers labor in a sugarcane field.

throne. Liliuokalani was the first woman in Hawaii's history to rule the islands. Her goal was to restore power and strength to the native Hawaiian royalty. When the queen tried to take control of her country, white business owners became nervous and angry. Led by Sanford B. Dole, they seized control of the government in 1893 and removed Liliuokalani from power. Dole, the son of an American missionary, headed the new provisional, or temporary, government. Although Liliuokalani appealed to the United States government for help, President Grover Cleveland refused to intervene. He did not approve of Dole's actions, however, and refused his request to annex the islands and bring them under U.S. control.

On July 4, 1894, the provisional government declared Hawaii a republic. Dole himself took on the role of president of the new Republic of Hawaii. The republic was an independent nation, free of ties to any other nation. Many in Hawaii — especially Hawaiian businesspeople — wanted the republic to align itself with the United States.

In 1900, the islands were annexed by President William McKinley. This brought Hawaii under U.S. control. In 1890, the islands became a U.S. territory, officially making all Hawaiian residents U.S. citizens. Once again, Sanford Dole played an important role, this time as the territory's new governor. As a U.S. territory, Hawaii was allowed a nonvoting representative in the U.S. House of Representatives.

Hawaii and the U.S. Military

In the late 1890s, Hawaii became an important U.S. military port. In 1898, the United States was fighting the Spanish-American War in the Philippines. Because of its proximity to the Philippines, Hawaii was an excellent spot for the United States to launch military operations. After Hawaii was annexed by the United States in 1898, the U.S. Navy chose Pearl Harbor, a natural port near Honolulu, as the site for its largest base in the Pacific. Workers began dredging the harbor, making it deeper for the huge

▲ King David Kalakaua, the immediate predecessor of Liliuokalani, was the first Hawaiian monarch to visit the mainland. He is shown here meeting President Ulysses S. Grant in 1874.

A Sunken Sub

In 2002, University of Hawaii researchers discovered a sunken Japanese midget submarine outside of Pearl Harbor. According to military reports, the 78-foot (24-m) sub was sunk just two hours before the Japanese attacked Pearl Harbor on December 7, 1941. The historic discovery may prove that the U.S. military actually fired the first shots against the Japanese in World War II.

battleships, destroyers, and other ships that would dock there. In December 1911, the USS *California* became the first U.S. warship to dock in Pearl Harbor. During the next three decades, Hawaii became the United States' most important military outpost in the Pacific.

Despite its importance to the U.S. military, many Americans had never heard of Pearl Harbor until December 7, 1941. Early that morning, Japanese airplanes flew over the harbor and bombed the U. S. Navy's Pacific fleet. During the attack, nineteen ships were sunk or damaged. One of the ships sunk was the USS *Arizona,* the largest ship in the harbor that day. The *Arizona* went to the bottom of the harbor with more than eleven hundred men trapped inside.

The Japanese attack killed more than twenty-three hundred people and crippled the U.S. Pacific fleet. The attack also brought the United States into World War II. On December 8, the United States declared war on Japan. Because of a treaty with Japan, Germany and Italy subsequently declared war on the United States.

The day after Japan bombed Pearl Harbor, Hawaii's governor declared a state of federal martial law. This gave complete control of Hawaii's government to the U.S. military. For nearly three years, the Hawaiian Islands were governed by the army.

Throughout World War II, Hawaii served as a supply base for battles in the Pacific. The islands were also an important training site for new troops. As a result of its strategic location, Hawaii continued to be a target for enemy attack. The islands of Hawaii, Maui, and Kauai were all shelled by enemy submarines during the war.

▲ On December 7, 1941, Japanese forces bombed Pearl Harbor. Ford Island Naval Air Station and the USS *Shaw* were two of the targets hit during the surprise attack.

DID YOU KNOW?

Hawaii has several other state nicknames, including Pineapple State, Youngest State, and Paradise of the Pacific.

Statehood and Beyond

After World War II, many Hawaiian residents campaigned for statehood. Prejudice against the large Japanese population living in the islands, however, posed a problem. In June 1959, more than 90 percent of all islanders voted for statehood. The U.S. Congress finally made Hawaii the fiftieth U.S. state on August 21, 1959.

In the 1960s, a new type of industry supplanted sugar and pineapple farming in Hawaii. That industry was tourism. During the following decades, Hawaii grew and changed to meet the challenges posed by this new industry. Today, tourism is the backbone of Hawaii's economy. Each year, millions of people from the U.S. mainland and around the world fly into Honolulu International Airport. High-rise hotels and resorts now dot the coastline. Tourism-related services employ a large number of the state's residents. Today, one of Hawaii's major challenges is to find a balance between development and preservation of the islands' natural beauty.

Some native Hawaiians still resent the islands' take-over by the United States. In recent years, a move for a sovereign, or independent, Hawaii has gained support among native Hawaiians. In 1993, the U.S. Congress and President Bill Clinton signed a resolution that apologized for the 1893 overthrow of the Hawaiian monarchy.

An Apology to Hawaii

In January 1993, the United States formally apologized to native Hawaiians for the "illegal overthrow" of the Hawaiian monarchy. The apology was signed by President Bill Clinton on the hundredth anniversary of the takeover. Part of the resolution read:

"The Congress ... apologizes to Native Hawaiians on behalf of the people of the United States for the overthrow of the Kingdom of Hawaii ... and the deprivation of the rights of Native Hawaiians to self-determination [and] expresses its commitment ... to provide a proper foundation for recon-ciliation between the United States and the Native Hawaiian people."

◄ Participants in and supporters of the Aloha March stand in front of the U.S. Capitol during a rally. The native Hawaiians are seeking an increase in sovereignty over the island state, a greater awareness of events surrounding the U.S. annexation of Hawaii, and a larger land base.

Many Cultures, One People

> Life in Hawaii is a song.
> — *Author Jack London, "Good-Bye, Jack!" 1902*

From 1990 to 2000, Hawaii's population grew by 9.3 percent. That figure is under the national average of 13.2 percent. In 1990, about 89 percent of all Hawaiians lived in urban areas. Honolulu, on the island of Oahu, is the state capital and the largest city in the state. Nearly half of the island's residents live in and around the big city. Since the time of Kamehameha I, the city has served as a government, commercial, and military center. Iolani Palace, the former royal residence, is located here, as are the office buildings of the Big Five businesses that once controlled most of Hawaii. Pearl Harbor naval base is located nearby. As a major tourism destination, the Honolulu area is home to seaside resorts, big hotels, and other services geared toward visitors. Honolulu's international airport and port are the busiest in the state.

Age Distribution in Hawaii
(2000 Census)

0–4	78,163
5–19	249,088
20–24	83,409
25–44	362,336
45–64	277,940
65 & over	160,601

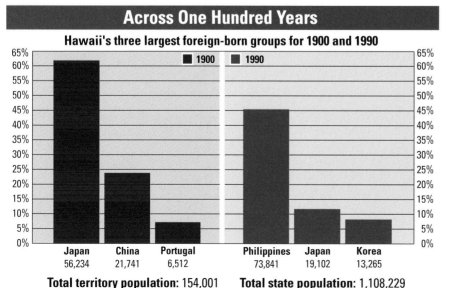

Across One Hundred Years
Hawaii's three largest foreign-born groups for 1900 and 1990

Legend: ■ 1900 ■ 1990

Japan	China	Portugal
56,234	21,741	6,512

Total territory population: 154,001
Total foreign-born: 90,780 (58.9%)

Philippines	Japan	Korea
73,841	19,102	13,265

Total state population: 1,108,229
Total foreign-born: 162,704 (14.7%)

Patterns of Immigration

The total number of people who immigrated to Hawaii in 1998 was 5,465. Of that number, the largest immigrant groups were from the Philippines (57.5%), China (8.8%), and Korea (5.2%).

Hilo, on the island of Hawaii, is the oldest city in the state. Although Hilo is the state's second most populated city, its population is just one-ninth the size of Honolulu's. Hilo's large port is an important trade and shipping center. Here, sugar and other goods from throughout the islands are exported to the mainland United States and around the world. Other big cities in Hawaii include Kailua, Kaneohe, and Waipahu on Oahu.

▲ One out of every nine people in Hawaii claims native Hawaiian ancestry.

Ethnicities

Hawaii is one of the most ethnically diverse states in the United States. There are no ethnic majorities or minorities here. In 1990, the three most common ancestry groups in Hawaii were Japanese, native Hawaiian, and Filipino.

The first people to settle in Hawaii were the Polynesians. For hundreds of years, they were the only people to live in the islands. Before European arrival, an estimated 300,000 native Hawaiians lived on the islands. Beginning in the early 1800s, people from the United States and other countries settled in the islands. They brought diseases that wiped out the native Hawaiian population. By 1919, fewer than 23,000 native Hawaiians were left on the islands.

DID YOU KNOW?

Hawaii has the highest percentage of Asian residents in the United States. It also has the third-highest number of Asian residents, although Hawaii ranks only forty-second in overall population. Only California and New York have more Asian residents.

Heritage and Background, Hawaii — Year 2000

▶ Here is a look at the racial background of Hawaiians today. Hawaii ranks thirty-ninth among all U.S. states with regard to African Americans as a percentage of the population.

Note: 7.2% (87,699) of the population identify themselves as **Hispanic** or **Latino**, a cultural designation that crosses racial lines. Hispanics and Latinos are counted in this category as well as the racial category of their choice.

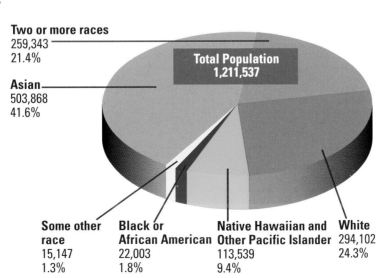

Total Population 1,211,537

Two or more races
259,343
21.4%

Asian
503,868
41.6%

American Indian and Alaska Native
3,535
0.3%

Some other race
15,147
1.3%

Black or African American
22,003
1.8%

Native Hawaiian and Other Pacific Islander
113,539
9.4%

White
294,102
24.3%

According to the 2000 census, 80,137 people living in Hawaii said they were entirely native Hawaiian. This number represents just 6.6 percent of the state's entire population.

During the mid-1800s, thousands of workers from China and Japan arrived in Hawaii to work on sugar plantations. Later, immigrants from the Azores, Norway, Germany, Puerto Rico, and Korea arrived to work in Hawaii. Over the years, Asian migration has continued. Since 1990, people from the Philippines, China, Korea, Vietnam, and Japan have accounted for more than 80 percent of all immigrants to Hawaii. In recent years, the largest number of immigrants have come from the Philippines. (In 1990, more than 45 percent of all immigrants to Hawaii came from the Philippines.) Today, the state has the largest percentage in the nation of residents claiming Asian heritage.

Education Levels of Hawaii Workers (age 25 and over)

Less than 9th grade	57,805
9th to 12th grade, no diploma	66,006
High school graduate, including equivalency	228,832
Some college, no degree or associate's degree	239,793
Bachelor's degree	142,493
Graduate or professional degree	67,548

▼ The skyline of Honolulu, Hawaii's capital and largest city.

Religion

Hawaii's religions are as diverse as its people. The earliest Hawaiians worshiped four main gods and a number of minor ones. Hawaiians believed that the gods created the earth, controlled the elements, and protected the people on the islands. Temples, called *heiaus*, were built out of lava and stone to honor the gods. The old religion died out after the death of Kamehameha I in 1819.

Today, many people in Hawaii are Roman Catholics. Catholics arrived in the islands shortly after the first Protestant missionaries. Another Christian faith that has played an important role in Hawaii is the Church of Jesus Christ of Latter-day Saints, whose followers are called Mormons. A group of Mormon missionaries arrived in Honolulu in 1855 and later established a small community on the island of Lanai. Other Christian groups in the state include the United Church of Christ, Baptists, and the Assemblies of God.

Another religion that has a large number of devotees in Hawaii is Buddhism. Buddhism was brought to the islands by the Asians who arrived to labor on the sugar plantations. In 1999, there were an estimated 100,000 Buddhists in the islands. Hawaii also has a small Jewish population.

Education

The first schools in Hawaii were established in 1820 by American missionaries. Two decades later, King Kamehameha III established the state's first public school system. Today, Hawaii is the only state in the nation to have its public school system run by the state instead of by individual counties or towns. A fourteen-member state board of education oversees Hawaii's educational standards. All children between the ages of six and eighteen must attend school. Just under 16 percent of these students attend private schools.

There are a number of public institutions of higher learning in Hawaii. One of these, the University of Hawaii, includes ten campuses. About 45,000 students attend school here each year. There are also a number of private universities in Hawaii, including Chaminade University and Hawaii Pacific University.

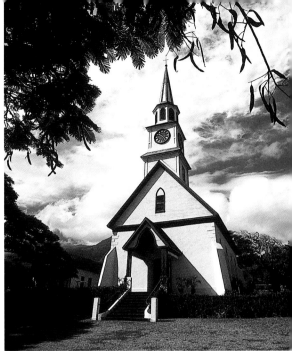

▲ Kaahumanu Church, the oldest on Maui, was first constructed in 1837. It was rebuilt in 1876.

The Hawaiian Alphabet

The Hawaiian alphabet was created by Protestant missionaries who came to the islands in 1820. The alphabet uses twelve letters to represent every sound made in the Hawaiian language — five vowels (a, e, i, o, u) and seven consonants (h, k, l, m, n, p, and w).

Hawaiian words include *ae* (yes); *alii* (chief); *aole* (no); *hale* (house); *haole* (White person); *hapa* (person of mixed ancestry); *kahuna* (wise person); *mahalo* (thank you); *mauna* (mountain); and *muumuu* (long dress).

A State of Islands

> What I have always longed for was the privilege of living forever away up on one of those mountains in the Sandwich Islands overlooking the sea.
> — *Mark Twain*, Letters from the Sandwich Islands, *1881*

Hawaii is a chain of more than 130 islands. Most of the islands are volcanic in origin. The state's total land area is 6,423 square miles (16,636 sq km). There are eight main islands. From west to east, the islands are Niihau, Kauai, Oahu, Molokai, Lanai, Maui, Kahoolawe, and Hawaii.

Highest Point
Mauna Kea
13,796 feet (4,205 m) above sea level

Niihau

The westernmost of the eight main islands is Niihau. At 72 square miles (186 sq km) in size, Niihau is the smallest of Hawaii's inhabited islands. The privately owned island is nicknamed the Forbidden Island because it is off-limits to everyone but invited visitors. The weather on Niihau is hot and dry, especially during the summertime.

Kauai

At 552 square miles (1,430 sq km), Kauai is the fourth-largest of the islands. Its terrain features volcanic peaks, deep valleys, and lush rain forests. The tallest mountain on the island is Kawaikini Peak. This extinct volcano measures 5,243 feet (1,598 m) above sea level. Kauai's fertile soil has earned it the nickname the Garden Island.

▼ *From left to right:* Waimea Canyon, Kauai; Hawaiian monk seal; Captain Cook Monument, Hawaii; a Hawaiian woman selling leis; native petroglyphs (rock carvings) on Hawaii; Pali lava flow, Volcanoes National Park, Hawaii.

Sugarcane and tropical fruits are grown on the island. The largest city on the island is Lihue.

Oahu

Oahu, the third-largest Hawaiian island, is 597 square miles (1,546 sq km). Called the Gathering Place, Oahu is the busiest island in Hawaii. Its largest city, Honolulu, is the state's capital and the center for most of Hawaii's big businesses. Oahu has many beautiful beaches, including world-famous Waikiki. The island, formed by two volcanoes, also offers green valleys and rugged mountains.

Molokai

Molokai, located between Oahu and Maui, is the fifth-largest island in Hawaii. It measures 260 square miles (673 sq km) in size. The world's tallest sea cliffs line the island's north shore. These enormous cliffs rise as high as 3,300 feet (1,006 m) above sea level. Molokai's main city and port is Kaunakakai. Often called the Friendly Island, Molokai is the most rural and least developed of the five biggest islands. Molokai's dry western section is home to cattle and sheep farms.

Lanai

The sixth-largest Hawaiian island, Lanai is 141 square miles (365 sq km) in size. The island terrain includes tall cliffs, fertile valleys, and sandy beaches. Its climate is mild and generally dry. Lanai was once called the Pineapple Island because nearly all the land here was part of a pineapple plantation. Now known as the Secluded Island, Lanai is being developed into a luxury resort. Lanai City is the main city on the privately owned island.

Maui

Known as the Valley Island, Maui is the second-largest island in the state. It totals 727 square miles (1,883 sq km).

Average January temperature
Honolulu:
  73.0°F (22.8°C)
Hilo: 71.4°F (21.9°C)

Average July temperature
Honolulu:
  80.8°F (27.1°C)
Hilo: 75.9°F (24.4°C)

Average yearly rainfall
Honolulu:
  23 inches (58.4 cm)
Hilo:
  128 inches (325.1 cm)

Average yearly snowfall
Honolulu:
  0 inches (0 cm)
Hilo: 0 inches (0 cm)

DID YOU KNOW?

Hawaii has more than 750 miles (1,207 km) of coastline. This is the fourth largest amount of all U.S. states.

Largest Lakes

Halalii Lake
860 acres (348 ha)

Kealia Pond
500 acres (202 ha)

Halulu Lake
371 acres (150 ha)

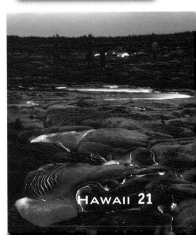

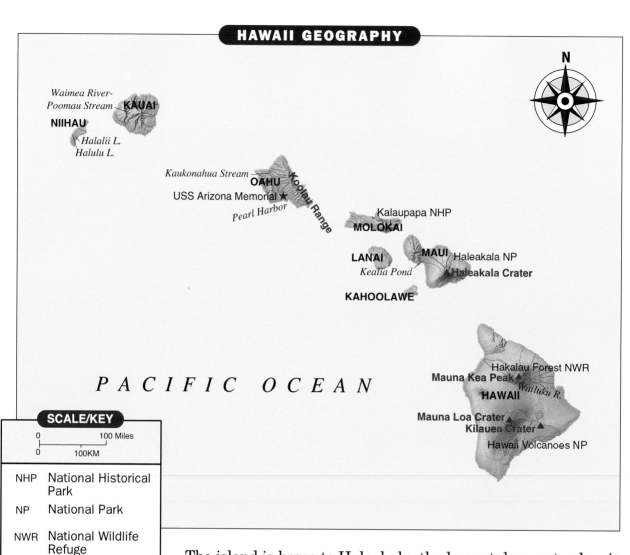

N

Waimea River- Poomau Stream — **KAUAI**

NIIHAU

Halalii L.
Halulu L.

Kaukonahua Stream — **OAHU**

USS Arizona Memorial ★

Koolau Range

Pearl Harbor

Kalaupapa NHP

MOLOKAI

LANAI   **MAUI** Haleakala NP
Kealia Pond   ▲Haleakala Crater

KAHOOLAWE

P A C I F I C   O C E A N

Hakalau Forest NWR
Mauna Kea Peak▲
Wailuku R.
HAWAII

Mauna Loa Crater▲
Kilauea Crater▲
Hawaii Volcanoes NP

SCALE/KEY

0	100 Miles
0	100KM

NHP	National Historical Park
NP	National Park
NWR	National Wildlife Refuge
★	USS *Arizona* Memorial
▲	Highest Point
▲	Important Peaks
▨	Mountains

The island is home to Haleakala, the largest dormant volcanic crater in the world. The island is rimmed with sandy beaches. Maui's climate is generally dry and sunny, although some high spots receive several hundred inches of rain annually.

Kahoolawe

Uninhabited Kahoolawe is just 45 square miles (117 sq km) in size. The dry island was once used by the U.S. military as a bombing target. Today, the federal government is cleaning up the island and its surrounding waters, but visitors are not allowed here without permission. Future plans for the island include a marine sanctuary.

Hawaii

Hawaii, nicknamed the Big Island, is the southernmost island in the state. It is also the largest and the youngest. Hawaii measures 4,028 square miles (10,433 sq km) in size and continues to grow. Five volcanoes built the island. One dormant volcano, Mauna Kea, is the tallest peak in the state. This inactive volcano towers 13,796 feet (4,205 m) above sea level. Each year, Hawaii's two active volcanoes, Mauna Loa and Kilauea, add more land to the island. The island's climate varies from place to place, with some spots receiving large amounts of rainfall during the winter.

Plants and Animals

Hawaii's plants and wildlife are very different from what is found on the U.S. mainland. More than twenty-five hundred different species of plants are native to the islands. Hawaii is also known for its many beautiful tropical flowers, including varieties of hibiscus, orchids, and bird of paradise. These brightly colored blooms are exported throughout the world.

The Hawaiian Islands are also home to many species of native birds. Some of these species are found nowhere else on Earth. Over the years, development and nonnative species have endangered many of Hawaii's birds. One-third of all birds listed by the United States as threatened or endangered are found in Hawaii.

Only two mammals are native to the islands: the hoary bat and the monk seal. Other animals, including rats, feral pigs, and feral goats, were all introduced by human settlers. The waters off Hawaii's coast are home to humpback whales, dolphins, and many other marine mammal and fish species.

Major Rivers

Kaukonahua Stream (South Fork)
33 miles (53 km)

Wailuku River
32 miles (51 km)

Waimea-Poomau
20 miles (32 km)

DID YOU KNOW?

The volcanoes that created the Hawaiian Islands are shield volcanoes. This type of gently sloping volcano is formed by quiet lava flows rather than explosive eruptions.

▼ Mauna Loa is one of the world's most active volcanoes. It last erupted in 1984. Volcanologists believe it may erupt at any time.

Sugar, Pineapples, and People

> The Earthly Paradise! Don't you want to go to it?
> Why of course.
> — *Author Henry Whitney*, Guide to Hawaii, *1875*

Over the years, Hawaii's economy has gradually shifted and evolved. At first, islanders depended upon forestry and farming. One of Hawaii's first industries was the harvesting and trading of sandalwood to visiting American merchants. Beginning in 1835, agriculture became the mainstay of Hawaii's economy. Huge sugarcane plantations were established, and for decades, "Sandwich Island sugar" was the region's major moneymaking crop. In the early 1900s, pineapples became a second chief crop when James Dole bought the island of Lanai to use as a pineapple plantation. By the 1990s, sugar and pineapple had diminished in importance. Nearly all the large plantations closed down because both products could be imported from other, cheaper sources. Today, the United States imports most of its sugar from the Dominican Republic, Brazil, and the Philippines, while pineapple, canned and fresh, comes from Mexico, Honduras, the Philippines, and Thailand.

Tourism and Transportation

Today, tourism is Hawaii's number one industry. In 2000, nearly seven million people visited the state. More than 63 percent of these visitors came from the U.S. mainland. Each year, tourists pump more than $10 billion into Hawaii's economy. The industry also provides more than 225,000 jobs for state residents. Hawaii's chief tourist islands are Oahu, Hawaii, and Maui. Kauai, Molokai, and Lanai are also trying to develop a larger tourist industry.

Most visitors to Hawaii arrive by airplane. The state has eleven airports to serve residents and visitors. The busiest

Top Employers (of workers age sixteen and over)
Services 48.9%
Wholesale and retail trade 15.4%
Federal, state, and local government (including military) 8.1%
Finance, insurance, and real estate 7.0%
Transportation, communications, and public utilities. . . 8.7%
Construction 6.0%
Manufacturing. . . 3.5%
Agriculture, forestry, fisheries, and mining. 2.3%

HAWAII ECONOMY

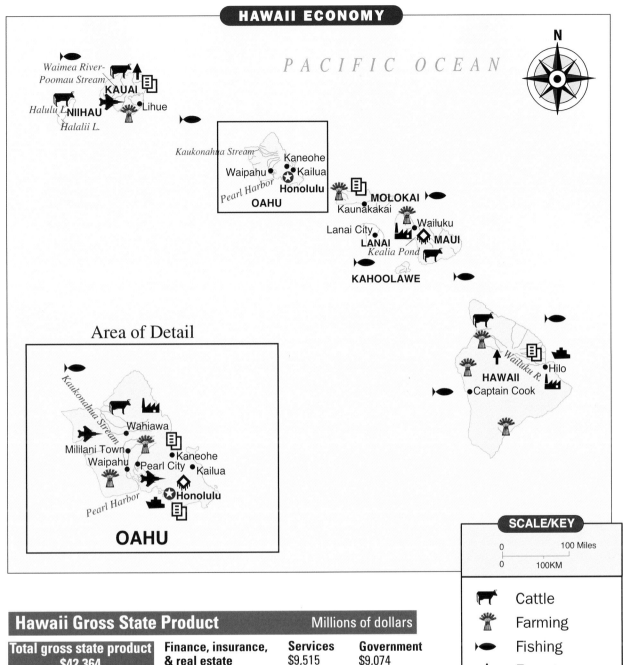

PACIFIC OCEAN

Waimea River-Poomau Stream

KAUAI

Lihue

Halulu L. **NIIHAU**

Halalii L.

Kaukonahua Stream

Kaneohe

Waipahu

Kailua

Pearl Harbor

Honolulu

OAHU

MOLOKAI

Kaunakakai

Lanai City

LANAI

Kealia Pond

Wailuku

MAUI

KAHOOLAWE

N

Area of Detail

Kaukonahua Stream

Wahiawa

Mililani Town

Waipahu

Pearl City

Kaneohe

Kailua

Pearl Harbor

Honolulu

OAHU

Wailuku R.

Hilo

HAWAII

Captain Cook

SCALE/KEY

0 — 100 Miles

0 — 100KM

- Cattle
- Farming
- Fishing
- Forestry
- Manufacturing
- Military
- Services
- Shipping
- Technology

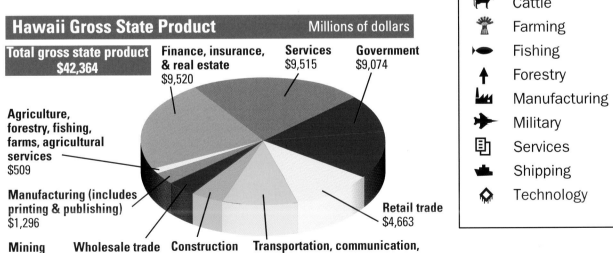

Hawaii Gross State Product — Millions of dollars

Total gross state product $42,364

Finance, insurance, & real estate $9,520

Services $9,515

Government $9,074

Agriculture, forestry, fishing, farms, agricultural services $509

Manufacturing (includes printing & publishing) $1,296

Mining $44

Wholesale trade $1,602

Construction $1,853

Transportation, communication, & utilities $4,288

Retail trade $4,663

HAWAII **25**

airport in the state is Honolulu International Airport.
Most international and domestic flights arrive here. Other
airports mainly handle travel between the islands. The only
islands that do not have commercial airports are Niihau
and Kahoolawe.

Water transportation is also important to Hawaii. Cruise
ships bring more than 38,000 visitors each year. Container
ships bring food and other goods and take sugar, canned
fruits and juices, and other exports back to the mainland.
Hawaii's main ports are Honolulu and Barbers Point on
Oahu, Hilo on Hawaii, and Kahului on Maui. The state also
has about 4,100 miles (6,600 km) of federal, state, and local
roads.

The Military

The military is another important part of Hawaii's
economy. During the Spanish-American War (1898) and
World War II (1941–1945), the islands were important bases
for American military operations. The military continues to
maintain a strong presence in Hawaii.

The armed forces own about 242,000 acres (97,937 ha)
of land in Hawaii, and more service people are stationed
here than in any other state. Oahu is the headquarters
of the military's Pacific Command. The Pacific Command
oversees military operations from the West Coast of the
United States to the east coast of Africa. About one-fourth
of all land on Oahu is held by the military. The island has
more than a hundred military installations, including radar
stations, naval bases, and airfields. Pearl Harbor, near
Honolulu, is U.S. Navy headquarters.

Agriculture, Forestry, and Mining

Agriculture accounts for just over 1 percent of Hawaii's
annual gross state product. Crops are the most important
part of this income. There are about 6,000 farms throughout

▲ Workers harvest
pineapples at one
of Hawaii's three
canneries.

The Pineapple Industry in Hawaii

In the late 1800s,
pineapple planters
began looking for ways
to preserve pineapples
so they could be shipped
to the mainland. In 1892,
the first pineapple
cannery was opened in
Waipahu on Oahu. In
1899, James Dole arrived
in Hawaii. The cousin
of politician Sanford
Dole, James Dole bought
the island of Lanai and
founded a pineapple and
produce franchise that
would spread throughout
the world. Dole himself
is remembered as the
"Pineapple King." By
the early 1960s, Hawaii's
nine canneries produced
80 percent of the world's
supply of canned
pineapple. A decade
later, however, the
industry was on the
decline, and only three of
these canneries survived.

Hawaii. The average farm size is 253 acres (103 ha). Sugarcane and pineapple remain the top two crops in the state. These two products account for 86 percent of all crop revenue in Hawaii. Other crops grown in the state include macadamia nuts, papayas, flowers and plants, and coffee. A smaller part of the agricultural income comes from livestock. Milk, cattle, eggs, hogs, and chickens account for just 15 percent of the total agricultural income.

Mining accounts for less than 1 percent of the annual gross state product. The most important mineral product in the state is stone, followed by cement, sand, and gravel.

▲ Waikiki Beach on the island of Oahu is one of Hawaii's most famous and most popular tourist spots. Thousands of visitors crowd its shores and hotels to enjoy Hawaiian sunshine and surf.

Manufacturing

Manufacturing accounts for about 3 percent of Hawaii's annual gross state product. The state's most important manufactured goods are processed foods, especially raw sugar, canned fruits, and canned juices. In 1999, the sale of raw sugar accounted for more than $129 million. Printing and publishing are also important parts of the total manufacturing income. Other Hawaiian industrial products include clothing, textiles, chemicals, furniture, and transportation equipment. Most industrial parks are located on the island of Oahu.

Made in Hawaii

Leading farm products and crops
Sugarcane
Pineapples
Macadamia nuts
Fruit
Flowers and plants
Coffee
Milk

Other products
Processed foods
Stone, cement, sand, and gravel
Printing and publishing
Apparel and textiles

Major Airports		
Airport	**Location**	**Passengers per year (2000)**
Honolulu International	Oahu	23,016,542
Kahului	Maui	6,191,245
Lihue	Kauai	2,883,472
Kona International	Hawaii	2,842,035
Hilo International	Hawaii	1,588,715

Hawaii's Government

> God hath made of one blood all nations of men to dwell on the Earth, in unity and blessedness. God has also bestowed certain rights alike on all men and all chiefs, and all people of the lands.
>
> — *Kingdom of Hawaii Constitution, 1840*

In 1950, the people of Hawaii adopted a constitution. This constitution went into effect in 1959, when Hawaii became the fiftieth U.S. state. Amendments to the constitution are proposed by Hawaii's legislature or by a constitutional convention. An amendment must be approved by a majority of the residents voting on the amendment. Those voting must represent a specific percentage of Hawaii's voters.

The system of government in Hawaii — just like that of the U.S. federal government — is divided into three branches: executive, legislative, and judicial. The executive branch administers laws, the legislative branch makes the laws, and the judicial branch interprets the laws.

The Executive Branch

The governor of Hawaii is the state's chief executive. The governor makes sure that state laws are carried out effectively and directs how money is collected and spent in the state. One of the governor's most important jobs is to appoint capable people to government offices. The governor appoints court justices and most members of the eighteen executive and administrative departments. These departments include Accounting and General Services; Budget and Finance; and Business and Economic Development and Tourism. Among the few executive positions that Hawaii's governor does not appoint are that of lieutenant governor and the state board of education members. The governor also selects people to serve on the state's many boards and commissions. All of the governor's appointments must be approved by the senate.

The Constitution

"We, the people of Hawaii, grateful for Divine Guidance, and mindful of our Hawaiian heritage and uniqueness as an island State, dedicate our efforts to fulfill the philosophy decreed by the Hawaiian state motto, 'Ua mau ke ea o ka aina i ka pono.'

"We reserve the right to control our destiny, to nurture the integrity of our people and culture, and to preserve the quality of life that we desire.

"We reaffirm our belief in a government of the people, by the people and for the people, and with an understanding and compassionate heart toward all the peoples of the earth, do hereby ordain and establish this constitution for the State of Hawaii."

— *Preamble to the Hawaii State Constitution, as amended in 1978*

Elected Posts in the Executive Branch		
Office	Length of Term	Term Limits
Governor	4 years	2 consecutive full terms
Lieutenant Governor	4 years	2 consecutive full terms
Board of Education Member	4 years	none

Another power held by the governor is the right to veto proposed legislation. In Hawaii, the governor can veto an entire bill or just certain sections of bills. The legislature can override the governor's veto with a two-thirds majority vote in both houses.

The governor is assisted by a lieutenant governor. The lieutenant governor is elected with the governor and must be from the same party. Should the governor be unable to serve for any reason, the lieutenant governor takes over.

The Legislative Branch

Hawaii's state lawmaking body is a bicameral legislature. This means that the legislature has two separate bodies. One part is the twenty-five-member Senate. The second part is the fifty-one-member House of Representatives. Hawaii's legislature is responsible for writing and passing new state laws. The legislature also approves the governor's state budget and allocates how state funds will be used.

The legislature meets annually in Honolulu beginning on the third Wednesday of January. This regular session continues for up to sixty days. Special sessions of the legislature may be called by the governor or by written request from two-thirds of both legislative bodies. These special sessions may last for up to thirty days. Both regular and special sessions can be extended for up to fifteen days at the request of the governor or two-thirds of both the House and the Senate.

▼ Construction on Hawaii's capitol building, located in Honolulu, was completed in 1969. The building and grounds around it were designed to reflect the state's unique geography, including its volcanoes, oceans, and palm trees.

The Judicial Branch

The judicial branch consists of the judges who preside over
Hawaii's courts. Each court is subject to review by a higher
court. Hawaii's highest court is the state supreme court.
The supreme court's five justices interpret the state laws
and decide if these laws adhere to Hawaii's constitution.
Chosen by the governor, the justices serve ten-year terms.
One of the five justices is chosen by the others to serve as
chief justice. The other four are known as associate justices.

The second-highest court in the state is the intermediate
court of appeals. This court has four justices. Below the
intermediate appellate court are the circuit courts. Most
civil and criminal trials in Hawaii take place in the circuit
courts. There are a total of twenty-nine judges in these
courts. Justices of the circuit courts are appointed by
the governor for ten-year terms. As with other state
appointments, the senate must approve of the governor's
choices. Other courts in Hawaii include district courts,
family courts, a tax appeal court, and a land court.

Local Government

Hawaii is the only state in the nation that does not have
incorporated municipalities. A municipality is a city, town,

State Legislature			
House	Number of Members	Length of Term	Term Limits
Senate	25 senators	4 years	No limit
House of Representatives	51 representatives	2 years	No limit

or village. Instead, the state is divided into four counties: Honolulu County governs the island of Oahu and various northwest islands; Hawaii County governs the island of Hawaii; Kauai County governs Kauai and Niihau; and Maui County governs Maui, Molokai, Lanai, and Kahoolawe. A fifth county, Kalawao, is run by the state Department of Health. It does not serve as a political unit and has no mayor or council.

Each county is governed by a mayor and a county council. Three of Hawaii's counties have a nine-member council. The fourth, Kauai County, has seven council members. Both the mayor and council members are elected by voting residents. Together, the mayor and the council members make sure the county runs smoothly. They oversee county services, such as fire, police, and emergency services. They also decide upon local land-development issues and local laws.

National Representation

Like all states, Hawaii has two senators in the U.S. Senate. Because of the state's small size and population, it has just two representatives in the U.S. House of Representatives. In 2004, Hawaii will retain four electoral college votes, the same as in recent elections.

Hawaii Politics

Before Hawaii became a state, Hawaiian voters usually elected Republican candidates to represent them. Since the 1960s, however, a major shift has occurred. Today, Hawaii is one of the most Democratic states in the nation. Hawaiians generally vote for Democratic presidential candidates; in 1998, 82 percent of all elected state legislators were Democrats. Members of this party also dominate local offices.

▶ Senator Daniel Inouye receives a Four Freedoms Award from Anne Roosevelt during a ceremony in Washington, D.C. The award, from the Roosevelt Institute, honors Americans whose careers reflect the ideals and commitment that define greatness in a democracy.

Famous Hawaiian Politicians

In 1959, Hiram Fong (above) made history when he was elected the first U.S. senator from the state of Hawaii. Fong was also the first U.S. senator of Asian descent. Fong, the child of Chinese immigrants, was born in Honolulu in 1907. He worked his way through college, eventually earning a law degree from Harvard University. During World War II, he served as a major in the U.S. Air Corps. He later served as a territorial legislator for fourteen years.

Daniel K. Inouye was selected to be the first U.S. representative from the state of Hawaii. Like Fong, Inouye had also served the United States valiantly during World War II. He was the first Japanese American to serve in the House. In 1962, Inouye again made history when he became the first American of Japanese descent to be elected to the U.S. Senate. In 2002, Inouye continued to serve his state and country in the Senate.

Something for Everyone

> Hawaii is not a state of mind,
> but a state of grace.
> — *Author Paul Theroux,*
> *writing in* The London Observer, *1989*

Hawaii is a tropical Pacific paradise that offers something for everyone. The sandy beaches, sunny days, and pounding surf attract swimmers, surfers, and sun worshipers from around the world. Nature lovers stroll through rain forests, dive off towering sea cliffs, and scale dormant volcanoes. They might even witness a volcanic eruption.

Those who want a unique cultural experience can have one without leaving the United States. That's because the fiftieth U.S. state can sometimes feel like an exotic, foreign land. Here, visitors can hear residents speaking both English and Hawaiian, the two official languages. Many Hawaiian words have become part of the daily dialogue. Visitors might also hear something called pidgin. Pidgin is a type of slang that combines English, Hawaiian, and Asian words. It developed over the years as a way for the various immigrant groups in Hawaii to communicate with one another. Visitors can also see a hula, a dance with ancient roots, and eat roast pig, fish, poi, and tropical fruits at a Hawaiian feast called a luau.

National Parks and Historical Sites

The Hawaiian Islands are rich in history. Visitors can trace the

▼ A statue guards a temple at Puuhonua O Honaunau National Historic Park.

development of the islands from their volcanic origins to the hustle and bustle of today's Honolulu. Traces of the many different cultures that have molded the islands' history can be found everywhere. On the island of Hawaii, visitors can see the birthplace of Kamehameha I. In Oahu, they can see Byodo-In, or Temple of Equality, a replica of a nine-hundred-year-old Japanese temple. Chinatown in Honolulu is a popular site for those interested in Hawaii's Chinese immigration. And visitors can also stand on the steps of Aliiolani Hale (House of the Heavenly Chiefs), where Sanford Dole announced the end of Hawaii's monarchy.

Hawaii is home to two national parks as well as several national historical sites and state parks. Kilauea and Mauna Loa, Hawaii's two active volcanoes, are protected in Hawaii Volcanoes National Park on the island of Hawaii. Here, visitors can watch lava oozing toward the sea and may even watch a volcanologist, a scientist who studies volcanoes, at work. Hawaii's second national park is Haleakala National Park on Maui. This park protects Haleakala, a dormant volcano.

Puuhonua O Honaunau National Historic Park on the island of Hawaii contains ancient temples, royal grounds, and a place where lawbreakers could seek sanctuary. Twenty-three royal chiefs are buried within one temple

▲ Volcanoes National Park on the Big Island is one of Hawaii's favorite tourist attractions. Spectators can walk on the active lava beds of Kilauea Volcano to observe one of Hawaii's most active volcanoes from close range.

Grand Canyon of the Pacific

Kauai's Waimea Canyon is known as the Grand Canyon of the Pacific. The canyon, carved out by the Waimea River-Poomau Stream, is 2,785 feet (849 m) deep. The canyon is located in Koke'e State Park, which features 45 miles (72 km) of hiking trails.

here. Another National Historic Park is Kalaupapa on Molokai, the site of a leprosy settlement since 1866. It was here that Father Damien, a Belgian priest, cared for people suffering from the deadly disease. Some people with leprosy, now known as Hansen's disease, still live here.

One of the most visited sites in Hawaii is Pearl Harbor. Each year, about 1.5 million people visit the USS *Arizona* Memorial located here. The memorial honors the more than 2,300 people who died during a Japanese attack on the harbor on December 7, 1941. Visitors can stop first at the memorial's visitor center, which includes a theater and a museum. Then they can take a boat ride out to the memorial, located over the sunken *Arizona*.

Libraries and Museums

Hawaii's first public library was opened in downtown Honolulu in 1913. Today, Hawaii's statewide library system includes about fifty branches throughout the islands. People with a library card can borrow and return materials at any of these branches. One special library is the Archives of Hawaii, which contains the most extensive collection of Hawaiian literature anywhere in the world.

Hawaii's museums contain some of the finest collections of Polynesian and Asian-Pacific culture that can be found

▲ The USS *Arizona* Memorial straddles the sunken hull of the *Arizona*. The memorial is one of the most visited sites in Hawaii. Oil continues to leak from the sunken battleship.

DID YOU KNOW?

Haleakala is the world's largest inactive volcanic crater. The dormant volcano last erupted about two hundred years ago. *Haleakala* is a Hawaiian word that means "House of the Sun." Ancient Hawaiians believed that the demigod Maui once trapped the Sun and kept it inside the mountain to give the island people more sunshine.

anywhere. The oldest museum in the state is the Bishop Museum in Honolulu. Opened in 1899, the museum features many amazing artifacts, including a feathered cloak worn by Kamehameha the Great. Another museum filled with history is Iolani Palace. The palace was the home of the Hawaiian monarchy from 1882 to 1893. It is the only royal residence in the United States. Other Hawaiian museums include the Honolulu Academy of Arts on Oahu, the Lahaina Whaling Museum on Maui, and the Kauai Museum on Kauai.

Communications

The first newspaper to be published in Hawaii was the Hawaiian-language weekly *Ka Lama Hawaii,* started in 1834. That paper was followed two years later by the first English-language newspaper, Honolulu's *Sandwich Island Gazette.* Today, there are six daily newspapers in Hawaii. The paper with the largest circulation is *The Honolulu Advertiser,* which is published daily and sold throughout the state. Other newspapers include Hilo's *Hawaii Tribune-Herald,* Kailua-Kona's *West Hawaii Today,* and Wailuku's *The Maui News.*

▼ The Bishop Museum was founded in 1899 to honor one of Hawaii's royal family members. Each year, thousands of people visit the museum, the oldest in Hawaii.

Several magazines are also published in Hawaii. *Honolulu* is a monthly periodical that appeals to Hawaii residents. *Hawaii Magazine*, published six times a year, is geared toward visitors. The state also has a number of radio and TV stations that serve Hawaiians and tourists alike.

▶ Polynesian dancing is an ancient musical tradition in Hawaii.

Music, Dance, and Theater

Two of the most distinctive features of Hawaii's culture are its music and dance. One instrument associated with Hawaiian music is the ukulele. This small guitar was introduced to the Hawaiian Islands by Portuguese immigrants. The Hawaiian name *ukulele* means "jumping flea." Two other types of guitars, slack-key and steel, were both developed in Hawaii. The steel guitar was invented in 1889 by Joseph Kekuku of Oahu.

The hula is an ancient dance form that originated hundreds of years ago with early Polynesian settlers. Hula includes dancing, *mele* (chanting), and drumming. To the ancient Hawaiians, the hula represented a way to keep old stories and legends alive. Today, the hula is still taught in special schools called *halau*.

Other types of musical experiences can be enjoyed at the Hawaii Opera Theatre and the Honolulu Symphony, both on Oahu. These are the two most prestigious musical companies in Hawaii. The Honolulu Orchestra, founded in 1900, is the oldest American orchestra west of the Rocky Mountains. Fine drama is represented in Hawaii, too. Kumu Kahua Theater, located on Oahu, produces plays by Hawaiian playwrights about Hawaiian life. Founded in 1971, it is the second-oldest Asian-American theater in the United States.

Sports

Many of Hawaii's sporting activities center on the waters of the Pacific Ocean. Surfing, swimming, cliff diving, windsurfing, and outrigger canoe paddling are all popular Hawaiian sports. Surfing originated centuries ago, with Hawaii's nobles. These wave-riding royals competed against each other, using huge surfboards that measured up to 24 feet (7.3 m) in length and weighed as much as 200 pounds (90.7 kilograms). Today, a number of major surfing competitions are held in the islands.

Although Hawaii has no professional sports teams of its own, the best players in the National Football League (NFL) travel to Honolulu each year to take part in the Pro Bowl. The Pro Bowl is held the weekend after the Super Bowl. Sumo wrestling, a sport with ancient Asian roots, is also popular among some Hawaiians. Sumo wrestling is one of Japan's oldest forms of martial arts. During a match, two large men struggle to knock one another out of a ring. The greatest sumo wrestlers are known as *yokozuna*. In recent years, some Hawaiian natives have dominated sumo wrestling. In 1993, Hawaiian Chad Rowan became a *yokozuna*. Rowan wrestles under the name Akebono.

▼ Entrants begin the 2.4-mile (3.9-km) swim segment of the Ironman Triathlon World Championship in Kailua-Kona. In addition to the swim, contestants bicycle 112 miles (180 km) and then run a marathon of 26.2 miles (42.2 km).

Hawaii Greats

Alexander Cartwright, known as the "father of modern baseball," loved Hawaii. Born in New York City in 1820, Cartwright pioneered the nine-player baseball team. In 1845, he helped found the first baseball team, the New York Knickerbockers, and played in the first organized baseball game. Sailing on his way home from the California Gold Rush in 1849, Cartwright stopped in Hawaii and decided to remain there. He was responsible for introducing baseball to Hawaii.

In a sport often associated with men, Paula Newby-Fraser proved that women could compete — and excel. Newby-Fraser won the Ironman Triathlon World Championship in Hawaii eight times — a record. She set a women's record in the event, finishing in eight hours and 55 minutes. Newby-Fraser, who was born in Zimbabwe, Africa, has been called one of the greatest all-around female athletes in the world.

Hawaii History-Makers

Hawaii ponoi Nana i kou, moi
Kalani alii, ke alii
"Hawaii's own true sons, be loyal to your chief,
Your country's liege and lord, the sovereign."
— *From "Hawaii Ponoi" by King David Kalakaua*

Following are only a few of the thousands of people who were born, died, or spent much of their lives in Hawaii and made extraordinary contributions to the state and the nation.

PRINCESS BERNICE PAUAHI BISHOP
PHILANTHROPIST

BORN: *December 19, 1831, Honolulu, Oahu*
DIED: *October 16, 1884, Honolulu, Oahu*

Bernice Pauahi Bishop (below) was the great-granddaughter of Kamehameha I and the last of his royal line. When she was nine, Bishop began to live with American missionaries living in Hawaii. Although strongly influenced by Western culture, she hated the racism that affected many native Hawaiians. In 1872, Bishop refused to become monarch after the death of her cousin, Kamehameha V.

Bishop may have wanted to avoid the increasing strife and conflict between the Hawaiian monarchy and the powerful American businessmen. During the final years of her life, she used her wealth and royal status to improve the lives of native Hawaiians. In her will, Bishop provided money for the founding of schools. Today an important museum bears her name.

QUEEN LILIUOKALANI (LYDIA KAMAKAEHA PAKI)
MONARCH

BORN: *September 2, 1838, Honolulu, Oahu*
DIED: *November 11, 1917, Honolulu, Oahu*

Liliuokalani was the first queen of Hawaii. She was also its last ruler. Liliuokalani became Hawaii's ruler after the death of her brother, King David Kalakaua, in 1891. She quickly angered the powerful white business owners who controlled much of Hawaii's finances and government. Two years after Liliuokalani became queen, the business owners staged a bloodless revolution and forced her from

power. Liliuokalani then turned to writing and translating Hawaiian poems. Her best-known creation is the Hawaiian song "Aloha Oe."

FATHER DAMIEN (JOSEPH DE VEUSTER)
MISSIONARY

BORN: *January 3, 1840, Tremelo, Belgium*
DIED: *April 15, 1889, Kalaupapa, Molokai*

Father Damien, a Roman Catholic missionary, arrived in Hawaii in 1865. Eight years later, Father Damien was chosen to head the leper colony on the island of Molokai. For the rest of his life, Father Damien worked closely with the people suffering from this disease, caring for them both spiritually and physically. He also petitioned the government for much-needed funds for the colony. In 1884, Father Damien contracted leprosy (now called Hansen's disease). He continued working on Molokai until his death in 1889.

SANFORD B. DOLE
LAWYER AND POLITICIAN

BORN: *April 23, 1844, Honolulu, Oahu*
DIED: *June 9, 1926, Honolulu, Oahu*

The son of American missionaries, Sanford Dole carved his own name in Hawaiian history. Dole studied law on the U.S. mainland before returning to the islands. Here, he became involved

in politics and was eventually appointed as a justice on the kingdom's supreme court. In 1893, Dole and other business leaders overthrew Hawaii's monarchy and took control of the government. Dole served as the first president of the Republic of Hawaii and as the first governor of the U.S. territory of Hawaii.

HIRAM BINGHAM
EXPLORER

BORN: *November 19, 1875, Honolulu, Oahu*
DIED: *June 6, 1956, Washington, D.C.*

Hiram Bingham was named for his grandfather, one of the first Americans to arrive in Hawaii in 1820. Bingham spent his childhood years in Hawaii before heading to the mainland to attend college. In 1906, he took up exploration, journeying throughout South America. In 1911, Bingham led an expedition that discovered the ruins of Machu Picchu, an ancient Incan city in Peru. Machu Picchu had long been dubbed "the lost city" because no trace of it could be found. After serving in the U.S. military during World War I, Bingham turned to politics. He was appointed lieutenant governor in Connecticut and later served eight years in the U.S. Senate. Bingham is buried in Arlington National Cemetery.

DUKE KAHANAMOKU
ATHLETE

BORN: *August 24, 1890, Honolulu, Oahu*
DIED: *January 22, 1968, Honolulu, Oahu*

Duke Kahanamoku was a native Hawaiian who excelled at swimming, surfing, and other water sports. During the 1912, 1920, and 1924 Olympic Games, Kahanamoku competed against other top swimmers. He won a total of five medals: three gold and two silver. He also focused international attention on the islands and their native people. In 1920, Kahanamoku formed one of the first surfing clubs at Waikiki. He also popularized surfing in California and Australia. Today, Kahanamoku is remembered as "the father of modern surfing." In 1984, he was inducted into the Olympic Hall of Fame.

GEORGE ARIYOSHI
POLITICIAN

BORN: *March 12, 1926, Honolulu, Oahu*

In 1974, George Ariyoshi was the first American of Japanese descent to be elected governor of a U.S. state. Ariyoshi served three terms as Hawaii's governor. During his twelve years in office, he worked hard to help the state grow and prosper. He encouraged economic development, especially of Hawaii's tourist trade. He also worked to protect the state's natural treasures. Since leaving office in 1986, Ariyoshi has remained active. In 1997, he

published his autobiography, *With Obligation to All*.

DON HO
ENTERTAINER

BORN: *August 13, 1930, Honolulu, Oahu*

Don Ho is known as Hawaii's most famous entertainer. Ho got his start during World War II, singing and playing the organ in bars and hotels. In 1966, he headed to the mainland, where he appeared in clubs and on TV shows, popularizing Hawaiian music throughout the nation. In 1996, Ho appeared in a movie called *Joe's Apartment*. He is best known for the song "Tiny Bubbles."

BETTE MIDLER
SINGER AND ACTRESS

BORN: *December 1, 1945, Honolulu, Oahu*

Bette Midler spent her childhood and teen years in Hawaii. After graduating from Honolulu High School, Midler moved to the mainland, where she made her mark as a singer and actress. Her first big break came in 1966, when she got a part in the Broadway show *Fiddler on the Roof*. Afterward, Midler released several records. Over the years, she has starred in such movies as *The Rose*, *For the Boys*, and *Hocus Pocus*. Midler received four Grammy awards for her singing and two Academy Award nominations for acting.

ELLISON ONIZUKA
ASTRONAUT

BORN: *June 24, 1946, Kealakekua, Hawaii*
DIED: *January 28, 1986, Cape Canaveral, FL*

When Ellison Onizuka boarded the space shuttle *Discovery* in January 1985, he made history. He was the first Hawaiian, the first Japanese American, and the first Buddhist astronaut in space. Onizuka, who served as an officer in the U.S. Air Force, joined the National Aeronautics and Space Administration (NASA) in 1978. Just one year after his history-making flight, Onizuka and six other crew members were killed when the space shuttle *Challenger* blew up shortly after takeoff.

ROBERT WYLAND
ARTIST

BORN: *July 9, 1956, Detroit, MI*

Robert Wyland, who makes his home in Oahu, is one of the world's leading environmental painters. The artist, who goes by the single name "Wyland," specializes in life-size drawings of whales, dolphins, and other underwater animals. Since the early 1970s, the artist's huge marine-life murals have livened up buildings all across the country. In 1992, Wyland completed the world's largest mural in Long Beach, California. A year later, he established the Wyland Foundation, an organization that tries to preserve Earth's oceans through art, education, and awareness.

STEVE CASE
BUSINESS EXECUTIVE

BORN: *August 21, 1958, Honolulu, Oahu*

In 1983, Hawaii-native Steve Case helped reorganize a failing online game company, Quantum Computer Services. Six years later, Case and Quantum launched America Online (AOL), an online service that provided users with news and other information for a monthly fee. By 1995, AOL had become the largest Internet services provider in the United States. Case is currently the chairman of AOL Time Warner, the world's leading media and entertainment company.

CHAD ROWAN (AKEBONO)
SUMO WRESTLER

BORN: *May 8, 1969, Honolulu, Oahu*

In 1993, Chad Rowan made sumo history. He became the first non-Japanese wrestler named *yokozuna*, the highest honor in sumo wrestling. Rowan's wrestling career began when he was nineteen years old. He left his home in Hawaii and moved to Japan to learn the art of sumo. When he began wrestling professionally, Rowan took the name *Akebono*, which means "sunrise" in Japanese. During the peak of his career, Rowan, who is 6 feet 8 inches tall (about 2 m), weighed more than 500 pounds (227 kg). He retired from the sport in 2001.

Hawaii
History At-A-Glance

A. D. 300
Polynesians from islands two thousand miles to the south begin to settle in present-day Hawaii.

1778
British captain James Cook becomes the first European to visit the Hawaiian Islands. Cook is killed in the islands the following year.

1782
Kamehameha I comes to power on the island of Hawaii after defeating the heir to the island's throne in battle.

1810
The Hawaiian Islands are united for the first time under the rule of Kamehameha I.

1820
The first American Protestant missionaries arrive.

1835
The first sugar plantation is established on Kauai.

1840
Kamehameha III establishes Hawaii's first public school system.

1848
The Great *Mahele*, or division, allows land to be sold to all people. Americans soon buy up huge tracts of the best land.

1852
Mass migration from Asia begins as thousands of Chinese laborers arrive to work on Hawaii's sugar plantations.

1875
Hawaii and the United States sign a treaty allowing Hawaiian sugar to be more easily imported to America.

1893
Hawaii's last monarch, Queen Liliuokalani, is overthrown and the Republic of Hawaii is formed the following year by Sanford Dole and other plantation owners.

1898
Hawaii is annexed by the United States.

1600 **1700** **1800**

1492
Christopher Columbus comes to New World.

1607
Capt. John Smith and three ships land on Virginia coast and start first English settlement in New World — Jamestown.

1754–63
French and Indian War.

1773
Boston Tea Party.

1776
Declaration of Independence adopted July 4.

1777
Articles of Confederation adopted by Continental Congress.

1787
U.S. Constitution written.

1812–14
War of 1812.

United States
History At-A-Glance

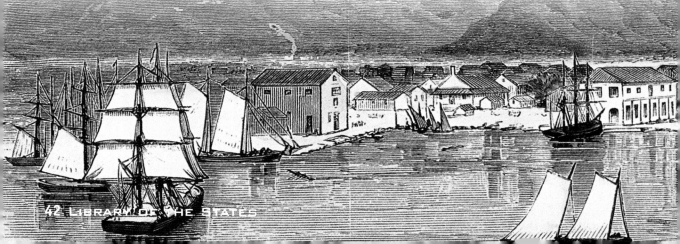

1900
Hawaii becomes a U.S. territory, making all its residents U.S. citizens.

1907
The University of Hawaii is founded at Manoa on Oahu.

1936
The *Hawaii Clipper,* a Pan American Airways plane, makes its first run from San Francisco to Oahu, introducing regular flights to the islands and launching Hawaii's tourist industry.

1941
Japanese troops attack Pearl Harbor. The following day, martial law is declared throughout the islands.

1946
A tsunami washes over Hilo, causing more than a hundred deaths and $25 million in damages.

1959
Hawaii becomes the fiftieth U.S. state.

1968
Hawaii amends its state constitution, adding a bill of rights.

1974
George Ariyoshi becomes the first Asian American governor in Hawaii — and the United States.

1983
Kilauea begins erupting. The eruption, which continues today, is the longest in the volcano's history.

1992
Hurricane Iniki sweeps through the islands, devastating Kauai and western Oahu.

1993
Congress passes and President Bill Clinton signs an apology to the native people of Hawaii for the kingdom's overthrow in 1893.

1800 — **1900** — **2000**

1848
Gold discovered in California draws eighty thousand prospectors in the 1849 Gold Rush.

1861–65
Civil War.

1869
Transcontinental railroad completed.

1917–18
U.S. involvement in World War I.

1929
Stock market crash ushers in Great Depression.

1941–45
U.S. involvement in World War II.

1950–53
U.S. fights in the Korean War.

1964–73
U.S. involvement in Vietnam War.

2000
George W. Bush wins the closest presidential election in history.

2001
A terrorist attack in which four hijacked airliners crash into New York City's World Trade Center, the Pentagon, and farmland in western Pennsylvania leaves thousands dead or injured.

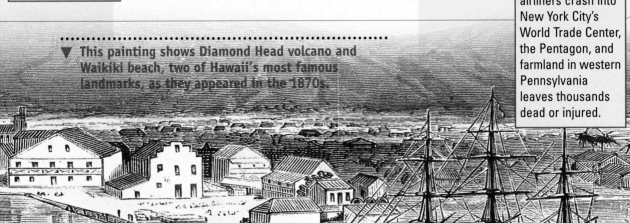

▼ This painting shows Diamond Head volcano and Waikiki beach, two of Hawaii's most famous landmarks, as they appeared in the 1870s.

HAWAII 45

Festivals and Fun for All

Check web site for exact date and directions.

Aloha Festivals,
Statewide

Hawaii's largest festival is also the only statewide celebration in the United States. Started in 1946 as a one-week celebration of Hawaii's heritage, activities now spread over a two-month period. Events include pineapple festivals, hula and singing contests, bed races, parades, and much more.
www.alohafestivals.com

Annual Ukulele
Festival, Oahu

Each year in July, the finest ukulele players in the world gather in Waikiki for the Annual Ukulele Festival. The festival features many entertainers, celebrities, and a children's ukulele orchestra with more than eight hundred members.
www.ukulele-roysakuma.com/uf.html

Hawaii Dragon Boat Festival, Oahu

Dragon boats compete in races at this annual festival in Honolulu that also features traditional Chinese arts and crafts.
www.chinatownhi.com

Hawaii State Farm Fair, Oahu

Held for more than fifty years, the fair features food, games, rides, and booths. The fair runs for three consecutive weekends.
www.hawaiistatefarmfair.org

Hawaiian International Billfish Tournament,
Island of Hawaii

The top marlin-fishing tournament in the world attracts anglers and spectators from around the world. The four-day competition takes place off the coast of Kailua-Kona.
www.konabillfish.com

International Festival of the Pacific,
Island of Hawaii

The Japanese cultural heritage is celebrated during this festival in Hilo, which features a large variety of events spread over several months. Highlights include a food feast, dance festival, parade, and tea ceremony.
www.international-festival.com

Ironman Triathlon World Championship, Island of Hawaii

Superfit athletes must swim 2.4 miles (3.9 km), bike 112 miles (180 km), and run 26.2 miles (42.2 km) — in 17 hours or less! The winner earns the title World Champion.
vnews.ironmanlive.com

Ka Molokai Makahiki, Molokai

This weeklong festival features such traditional Hawaiian games as *huki huki* (tug-of-war), *ulumaika* (lawn bowling), and *uma* (arm wrestling). Traditional music and dancing are also part of the fun festivities.
www.molokai-hawaii.com

King Kamehameha Celebration Floral Parade, Oahu

Floats decorated with fresh flowers, marching bands, and dancers celebrate the first king of the Hawaiian Islands.
www.state.hi.us/dags/kkcc

Made in Hawaii Festival, Oahu

The very best in Hawaiian-made products are on display during this three-day event. Held each year in Honolulu, the festival attracts artisans and other merchants from around the state. Visitors can purchase a wide variety of items, including tropical fruits, handmade crafts, gourmet food, and plants and flowers.
www.madeinhawaiifestival.com

Merrie Monarch Hula Festival, Hawaii

Hawaii's largest hula competition highlights this weeklong festival of cultural events.
www.merriemonarchlive.com

....

▶ A float in the King Kamehameha Celebration Floral Parade.

Moanikeala Auana Hula Festival, Oahu

Some of the youngest hula dancers from around the state come to the Polynesian Cultural Center to compete against each other. The competition is part of the Na Ka Mahina Malamalama Hawaiian Festival.
www.hoalahawaii.com

NFL Pro Bowl, Oahu

This face-off between the National Football League's best players takes place each year in Aloha Stadium.
www.nfl.com/probowl/index.html

Red Bull Cliff-Diving Championships, Lanai

High divers compete on the towering cliffs of Kaunolu National Historic Landmark for the chance to be named best in the world. From the top of these cliffs, native Hawaiian warriors plunged into the sea to prove their bravery and loyalty to their chief. Spectators come by boat to witness the free-falling fun.
www.redbullcliffdiving.com

Vans Triple Crown of Surfing, Oahu

These three surfing events attract wave riders from all around the world.
www.triplecrownofsurfing.com

Books

Allen, Thomas B. *Remember Pearl Harbor: American and Japanese Survivors Tell Their Stories*. Washington, D.C.: National Geographic Society, 2001. First-hand accounts of the attack on Pearl Harbor.

Feeney, Stephanie, and Ann Fielding. *Sand to Sea: Marine Life of Hawaii*. Honolulu: University of Hawaii Press, 1989. Photographs of underwater animals and plants liven up this fascinating book.

Kalakaua, King David. *The Legends and Myths of Hawaii: The Fables and Folk-Lore of a Strange People*. Rutland, VT: Charles E. Tuttle, 1972. Hawaii's last king, David Kalakaua, retells the ancient legends and stories of his ancestors. First published in 1888, this book by Hawaii's last king recounts ancient Hawaiian legends and stories.

Liliuokalani, Queen. *Hawaii's Story by Hawaii's Queen*. Rutland, VT: Charles E. Tuttle, 1991. Hawaii's last queen tells the story of Hawaii and her ancestors in this book, first published in 1898.

Rumford, James. *Ka-hala-o-puna, ka u'i o Manoa: The Beauty of Manoa*. Honolulu: Manoa Press, 2001. A beautifully illustrated version of an ancient Hawaiian tale about a rainbow girl.

Web Sites

▶ Official state web site
www.hawaii.gov

▶ Official state tourism web site
www.gohawaii.com

▶ Official city and county of Honolulu site
www.co.honolulu.hi.us

▶ Hawaiian Historical Society site
www.hawaiianhistory.org

Films and Documentaries

Atkins, Paul. *Hawaii: Strangers in Paradise*. National Geographic Society, 1991. Witness how the introduction of nonnative species has impacted Hawaii's native wildlife.

Atkins, Paul, and DeGruy, Michael. *Hawaii: Islands of the Fire Goddess*. Time Life Video, 1988. This video describes the evolution of Hawaii's islands.

Ducat, Vivian. *The American Experience: Hawaii's Last Queen*. WGBH Boston, 1997. Queen Liliuokalani's life and legacy are explored in this hour-long video.